HISTORY in a HURRY

Roundheads and Cavaliers

written and drawn by
JOHN FARMAN

MACMILLAN
CHILDREN'S BOOKS

Ancient China
Ancient Egypt
Ancient Greece
Aztecs
Dark Ages
French Revolution
Industrial Revolution
Middle Ages
Romans

Roundheads
  and Cavaliers
Stone Age
Stuarts
The Future
Tudors
Victorians
Vikings
Wild West

All **HISTORY** in a **HURRY** *titles can be
ordered at your local bookshop or are available by post
from Book Service by Post (tel: 01624 675137).*

First published 1999 by Macmillan Children's Books
a division of Macmillan Publishers Limited
25 Eccleston Place, London SW1W 9NF
Basingstoke and Oxford

Associated companies throughout the world

ISBN 0 330 37646 2

1 3 5 7 9 8 6 4 2

A CIP catalogue record for this book is available from the British Library.

Printed and bound in Great Britain by Mackays of Chatham plc, Kent

☁ CONTENTS

🌬️ OFF WE GO!

As a way of settling a nation's differences, civil wars are rather handy, but can be a bit dodgy if you happen to get in the way. The Civil War of the 17th century was by far the nastiest in Britain's history* and seems to have acted as a bit of a lesson to all who followed.

Recipe for Civil War
Take:
• *One cocky king.*
• *One fed-up parliament.*
• *One megalomaniac (look it up) military leader.*
• *A whole load of people who insist that their particular way of worshipping God is the only one worth bothering with.*
Stir in a country north of the border, that continually waves its fist at those south of the border.
Finally, add a Europe desperate to see the English in the deepest trouble possible, and – hey presto! – you have a truly explosive cocktail.

This magnificent volume attempts to take you through the major whys and wherefores of the English Civil War (and what actually happened) without getting bogged down with all the boring bits that teachers always seem to go on about.

By the way, don't worry about all those silly comments at the bottom of the pages: it's just my editor, Susie (Ed for short), trying to make my job more difficult.

* We've only had a couple! Ed

Chapter 1

THE MYSTERY OF
⚘⚌ *GOD'S WAYS...*

Throughout this book you'll notice the same religions – Catholicism, Protestantism, Puritanism, etc. – keep cropping up. Seeing as God was at the centre of all the fuss, I reckon it might be a bit helpful to tell you the difference (as far as I can work out) between them. I'll list them all in alphabetical order just in case you think I've got favourites (I don't want another civil war on my hands!).

– DON'T BLAME ME!

Anglicanism

The Anglican approach was formed by the Church of England during the Protestant (see *Protestant*) Reformation (see *Reformation*). It is distinguished by the Confession of Faith or the Thirty-Nine Articles of Faith of 1571, and the Liturgy, otherwise known as the book of Common Prayer, of 1559. Anglicanism is still the main religion in England today.

Catholicism

Originally this meant everyone who believed in Jesus. These days we refer to it as the Roman Catholic church because of the Roman stranglehold on all religion before the Reformation (see *Reformation*). The Pope is the head of the Roman Catholic church, and is seen as God's Representative On Earth. He is supposed to be directly descended from Jesus's best mate St Peter the Apostle (if you can call a 'best mate' someone who denies knowing you three times when the going gets rough).

JESUS WHO?

ST PETER

Roman Catholics go a bundle on saints, and tend to pray to saints, who then pass on the message to God. Their churches are full of incense (to help waft the prayers heavenwards), pictures (mostly of Jesus's mum, Mary), lots of gold decoration, etc. Their vicars are called Fathers and wear frillier frocks than the Anglicans.

Episcopalianism

An 'episcopy' means government by bishops, and when a bunch of Protestant people signed a covenant to get rid of the bishops, the ones that didn't sign were called the Episcopalians. They liked their bishops and so they kept 'em. (The ones that *did* sign were called the Covenanters, and were mostly Presbyterians. (See *Presbyterianism*.))

Presbyterianism

A Protestant (see *Protestantism*) church associated mostly with Scotland. Presbyterianism means that all the clergy (people who run it) are equal, that there is no difference between the priest and his audience (congregation) and that the whole thing is governed by the church elders, rather than by the bishops (see *Episcopalianism*).

Protestantism

Protestant is the name given to the Christians that aren't Roman Catholic (see *Catholicism*). A Protestant is someone who at one stage or another gives a solemn declaration of his beliefs or convictions (confirmation). He believes that he is only answerable to God and not some big-deal representative of God on Earth (the Pope). What are Protestants protesting about? Nobody seems to know. My encyclopedia says, and I quote, that 'a protest usually contains some negative association, but Protestantism is negative only in its positive consent.' *You what?* It doesn't sound that firm a rock to found a whole religion on, but who am I to say?* I think it originally meant that the Protestants were always getting their knickers in a twist about the constant infiltration of Roman Catholic habits into their nice plain lives. These habits were referred to

* Exactly. Ed

as High Church, while the Low Church people like their religion plain (no sauce?).

Puritanism

The title Puritan was the nickname given to a large group of Low Church Protestants, who didn't think that the Reformation (see *Reformation*) had gone far enough, and that it still kept too much Roman Catholic showmanship and rituals (bells, smells and stuff). They were a very serious bunch who weren't too happy about anything that looked like it might be too much fun. Their clothes, therefore, were very plain, as were all aspects of their lives.

Reformation*

Don't go thinking that the term *Reformation* actually means reformation, i.e. that it actually reformed something. It should read 're-formation', because it represented the huge move in the 16th century to re-form (i.e. rebuild) the Church after the Romans had taken it over. Everyone had had enough of all the rude and corrupt goings-on amongst the Roman Catholic nuns and monks, who were using religion as a fab cover for all their dirty dealings.

Quakers

Also known as the Society of Friends, they were a group of Protestants who organized their own Church, deciding to do away with all oaths, paid ministers and tithes (demands for money). The only other major difference I can identify was that they refused to take off their hats when they met each other. I also reckon the Quakers invented porridge (Quaker Oats, anyone?).

* The Reformation is not a religion. Ed
I know – it just seemed like it needed explaining. JF

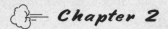
DOWN WITH THE KING!
(A BIT OF BACKGROUND)

To get some idea what the famous Civil War of 1642 was all about, it might be some help to have a look at the chap who caused it. Actually he didn't actually cause it, but it was all the things he did that caused other people to actually cause it. The guys who actually cau—*

King Charles I's Dad

Little Charles I had quite a happy childhood. His daddy was King James, the first person to be king of England and Scotland at the same time. He'd become the wee kinglet of the Scots (James VI) when a mere baby and became boss of them both (James I of England) with the Union of Crowns in 1603 (all described in my jolly good book – *Stuarts*, available at most refined bookshops). James VI was the first of the illustrious Stuart dynasty.

* Please get on with it. Ed

Useless Fact No. 871

When James I – or James VI, whichever you prefer – died, his son Charles, 24 (that's *not* Charles the 24th, that's his age), gave him a magnificent funeral, but didn't seem to care whereabouts in Westminster Abbey his dad was actually buried. James's body was not found until Victorian times when he was discovered sharing a tomb with Henry VII (his great-great-grandad). How cosy! Nobody knows how he got there.

His Mum

Charles I's mother was the affectionate and gay (if somewhat stupid) Anne of Denmark. She had lavished all her love and attention on his brother Henry, who just happened to be all the things Charles wasn't – good-looking, caring, brave, dashing, dignified, graceful – a seventeenth-century Prince Charming (in other words – a right goody-goody). Luckily for our Charlie, Henry died of typhoid in 1612, much to the dismay of his ma and the whole nation: being the elder brother, Henry was first in line to be kinged. Charles tried hard to be like his dead brother (well – apart from being dead, of course), and *not* like his dead dad, who'd been disliked for his coarse lifestyle, his court 'favourites' and his complete lack of personal hygiene (he stank to high heaven). Charles, in direct contrast, became known for his over-the-top fastidiousness in almost every aspect of his short life.* Like his father, however, he did think that he'd been placed on the throne by God himself (after He'd finished creating the world and stuff, naturally) and was therefore also, as head of the church, God's top man on earth. Again, just like his pa, Charles reckoned that Parliament was only there to give the OK to all his decisions and give him as much cash as he wanted, when he wanted it – which, I must admit, sounds OK to me.

Although Charles took his job as king quite seriously, you must remember that back in those still-quite-medieval days, it was of very little importance whether his subjects approved or disapproved of what he did or said. The only thing they could be sure of was that Charles would enforce his words with as much might and muscle as he could muster (let's face it, there's hardly any point being king otherwise).

War in Europe

At this time there was a humdinger of a war going on throughout Europe (called the Thirty Years War) which was basically about God – or, should I say, about all the different ways of worshipping him: Catholic, Protestant, Presbyterian, etc. (See Chapter 1.)

Charlie's dad, James, though dead grubby and dissolute, had been no fool, and had tried to keep on the right side of everyone by marrying off his daughter Lizzie to some German prince or other . . . to keep at least the Germans happy.

---

* Don't give the end away. Ed

Useless Fact No. 874
Lizzie (Elizabeth) was our Queen Elizabeth's great-great-great-great-great-great-great-great-great-grandmother.

He then tried to hitch his boy Charles to a Catholic Spanish princess . . . to keep the Spaniards happy. The official story was that it was *our* Protestant Parliament that was not too thrilled about an alliance with the Catholics, but it turned out to be the prospective bride, Maria Anna, who actually pulled out cos she didn't want to marry Charles.

Anyway, it all went pear-shaped: just two years later, James and England were at war with Spain. His reign, understandably, ended in total disaster. James was later labelled 'the wisest fool in Christendom'.

Useless and Inexplicable Fact No. 877
Every cloud has a silver lining. When the somewhat embarrassed prince returned to London from his failed marriage mission to Spain, there were mass celebrations to welcome him. A cartload of criminals on their way to be hung were suddenly pardoned as an act of goodwill to all men. I bet they were fans for ever.

King Charlie

It was said that, being a Scotsman, old James didn't understand the English – but his poor son Charles didn't understand the English *or* the Scots (or the Irish or the Welsh come to that), and boy, was he to prove it.

In 1625 he was persuaded to marry the Catholic king of France's 15-year-old sister, Henrietta Maria (hands across the sea and all that), but that went wonky as well, for within no time at all we were at war with France (as well as Spain).

Useless Fact No. 880

Charles didn't even turn up at his own wedding, and got his best friend the Duke of Buckingham to stand in for him at Notre Dame Cathedral in Paris (I hope that was all he did for him – nudge, nudge!*).

Parliament was soon well miffed with Charles and his poncy and precocious French wife. In fact, they were fed up with the whole Royal family, and it wasn't long before they were all trading blows with each other. It went a bit like this.

Parliament vs. King

First of all, Parliament had a pop at Charles's Catholic missus, saying he should never have married her (actually, they were not far from the truth – she was a bit of a pain in the *derrière* and buck-toothed into the bargain).

To follow up, in 1625, they took away the king's right to collect all tax on imports for ever and ever (they only let him have a year's worth).

Worse still, they only awarded him £140,000, a fraction of the money he needed for his brand new war with Spain.

* We'll have less of that, thank you. Ed

Useless Fact No. 883

The war turned out to be a catastrophe for England. The 10,000-strong but hopelessly ill-equipped navy failed to capture Cadiz and couldn't even get their hands on the Spanish treasure fleet. They came home with their sails between their legs.*

King vs. Parliament

Charles volleyed by raising a loan (by force) and banged up anyone who refused to cough up. Parliament, heavily backed by public opinion, retaliated by forcing him to sign a Petition of Right in 1628 which stated that any tax or loan raised without their say-so was illegal.

Charles hesitated for a second and then delivered the ultimate parting shot. With the backing of the Archbishop of Canterbury (William Laud) and Thomas Wentworth (later the brilliant Earl of Strafford), he dissolved Parliament altogether in 1629 and said that he'd do without, thank you very much. This hacked them off big-time, as you might imagine, especially when you consider that up till then no parliament could ever have been got rid of without its own consent. When tricksy Charles made a proclamation forbidding anyone to even talk about forming another one, and saying that from then on he would answer only to God, he'd obviously won hands down . . . or had he?

Cash on Demand

It must be said that Parliament in those days wasn't anything like the fine, conscientious and sophisticated debating society it is today (ho-ho). For starters, it only met now and again and was usually only called up when the king or queen needed cash

* Not *that* old joke. Ed

to fight a war, build a fleet or buy a couple of new frocks (queens, that is).

Without any money coming in from Parliament, Charles was forced to pluck England out of the war and the humiliated natives had to watch as their neighbours France and Holland became even more massively powerful. Quick-thinking as ever, Charles decided to raise taxes in every way possible, using his clever lawyers to find loopholes in the laws, as well as flogging titles to anyone who could stump up the hard cash (don't be fooled – much of the English aristocracy started this way, whatever they may tell you).

Three Ways to Make Yourself Unpopular

Our Charles, never one to miss a trick, came up with an idea that made it compulsory for anyone whose land brought them in more than £40 a year* to buy a knighthood – a very expensive business.

COULD YOU PAY ON THE WAY OUT?

* That rules you out then, Mr Farman. Ed

At the same time he cleverly stole masses of land by claiming that a load of existing titles were invalid.

Best of all, he invented the fabbo 'Ship Money', a special tax on all the coastal counties (and then later, the inland counties) to help pay for the navy.

Finally,* just to really put the boot where it hurt most, he gave special trading rights to all his best pals and courtiers, including the Duke of Buckingham, the greatest favourite of the lot (he'd been his dad's favourite too).

Charles Goes it Alone

The king managed to do without Parliament for over eleven years (1629–1640) supported by the aforementioned Earl of Strafford, Archbishop Laud – and a load of others who would later scarper abroad when the going got tough. If only he'd realized it, Strafford could have been his one hope, but sadly Charles never really liked or trusted him (actually he couldn't stand him, but don't tell anyone I told you).

By the way, in 1633, Charles had been crowned king of Scotland (as well) – much to their disgust. (Political union between Scotland and England wasn't fully established until 1707.)

Useless Fact No. 886

Laud and Strafford pushed through the now famous and much envied (especially by our Royals, I bet) policy of 'Thorough' which basically gave the king the right to do anything he darn well pleased. Thoroughly satisfactory.

Punishing the Puritans

But then Charles did something rather silly, which was eventually to contribute to his downfall. The Puritans (hard-

* That's *four* ways, not three. Ed

line English Protestants who thought the Anglicans 'too Catholic') had been giving him problems for some time. Through his dead strict High Church Anglican Archbishop of Canterbury (Laud), he authorized their severe persecution, until, in 1630, a load of them decided they'd had enough and jumped into a bunch of ships (the *Mayflower* was one of 'em) and high-tailed it off to the States (except it wasn't called that then) where they founded Massachusetts, Connecticut and Ben and Jerry's Ice Cream.*

The ones that didn't go, and weren't dead, obviously harboured a bit of a grudge . . .

Now the Presbyterians

With that under his belt, Charles daftly had a go at the Presbyterian Scots (rather him than me) making them use his brand new English Prayer Book in 1637 (it had also upset the Puritans), and forcing them to worship God in the same way

* I don't think so somehow. Ed

as his Archbishop Laud. This caused a riot in Edinburgh and a right rumpus throughout Scotland.

The Covenanters

An assembly of angry Presbyterians was formed in Glasgow, without the king's permission, and signed the Scottish National Covenant in 1638. The Covenant was an agreement to resist the introduction of Charles's beloved 'episcopy' (the ruling of the Church by bishops) and indeed to keep the blighters out of Scotland altogether. This was to be the cause of what was to be nicknamed the 'Bishops' Wars'. And it was getting hold of the money to pay for the Bishops' Wars that caused Charles such problems.

Charles Gets Tough

When the Scots refused to do as their king demanded, and began revolting all over the place, Charles was understandably miffed. In 1640, much to the distress of his English subjects, who by then thought he was losing the plot big-time, he sent a large army up north to teach 'em a lesson. Everyone (including the Scots) thought it would be a walkover, but by the time the English troops arrived they were knackered by the long walk, lack of decent grub and bad weather. All Charles's advisors thought he should give up and make a deal, especially the Earl of Strafford who'd been away in Ireland organizing a Catholic army. Strafford told Charles that if by any chance those dreaded Covenanters (as they were labelled) won, it would be the end of his supreme power.

In the end Charles had to give in and the Scots, surprised at the lack of resistance, invaded England instead and occupied Northumberland and Durham. There they sat, twiddling their thumbs, until Charles made a deal with them which included allowing them to stay in all the land they'd managed to pinch, plus all their expenses, to the tune of £850 a day, while they were there. The other part of this deal included the setting up of a new Parliament – to authorize the payment of the Scots – but this time one that couldn't be wound up at the drop of hat.

Useless Fact No. 888

Not content with upsetting the Scots, Archbishop Laud ordered the ears to be lopped off three English intellectuals who'd been distributing pamphlets against Charles's new regime..

Tricky Charles

But even though the wily king agreed to all the Scots' new demands, he most definitely had his fingers crossed, believing that, through God, something would turn up (like the Scots falling out with each other) to get him out of this new mess. And a right real mess it became.

Downhill Slide

Instead of things getting better, they got much worse, as, by now, absolutely everyone distrusted absolutely everyone else. The Long Parliament (as it was called) was determined to regain all the powers (particularly the right to hire and fire who they pleased) that they'd lost to the king, who they now regarded as 'irresponsible' (I imagine that was the polite word).

They started by arresting his right- and left-hand men, Earl Strafford and Archbishop Laud, and made the king sign their execution warrants.

Useless Fact No. 890

When Strafford (known as 'Black Tom Tyrant' to the common folk) was executed at Tower Hill, his head was waved on a pike to a hysterical baying mob.

It was at this time that it also came to light that Charles had been trying to do deals with the Irish Catholics, the Spanish Catholics and even the Pope, in an effort to get the cash necessary to finance the invasion of Scotland.

The Grand Remonstrance

In November 1641 a 'Grand Remonstrance' (a kind of protest vote) against the king was carried in the House of Commons – but only by a small majority. Clearly Parliament was also divided in opinion. First they abolished episcopy (rule by the bishops) and then ordered a complete reformation of the Church. All very well, but that too was only passed by the smallest majority. They then took over the army and navy. All of this was simply too much and Charles finally flipped. With a group of surly soldiers behind him, he marched into the House of Commons and tried to arrest the leader of parliament, John Pym (nicknamed 'the King'), and his cronies, all of whom ran away and hid in the City of London.

Was the actual king going round the bend? Pym's parliament certainly thought so. When Charles practically declared war on his own people it underlined their worst fears.

Useless Fact No. 892

On 30 December a nasty fight broke out between a mob of rowdy teenagers – forerunners of lager louts – just out for a fight, and a bunch of army officers who were on their way home from supper with the king. The officers goaded the apprentices by calling them 'roundheads' (because of their short haircuts) and the apprentices replied with taunts of *cavaliero* (after the Spanish soldiers who were England's and the Protestants' natural enemies). 'Roundhead' and 'Cavalier' were to become the official nicknames for the soldiers of the two sides:

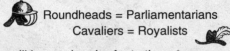

Roundheads = Parliamentarians
Cavaliers = Royalists

So now you'll know when I refer to them.*

* I thought Cavalier came from cavalry? Ed
No one really knows. Ssh! JF

Ban the Bishops

Although Archbishop Laud was still in the Bloody Tower awaiting head removal (they kept him waiting four long years), his strict High Church version of religion was still quite popular in some places.

In 1640 all the most important people, including clergy, wealthy farmers and the gentry, had decided (egged on by those furious Covenanting Scots) that the whole way that the Church was governed needed a right shake-up. This included getting rid of bishops (again!), getting rid of that blinking Prayer Book which they called, rather excessively I think, 'noisome and stinking in the nostrils of God', getting rid of those crazy Catholic customs like Easter and Christmas and getting rid of all those pretty (if you like that kind of thing) stained-glass windows.

It didn't take a genius to realize that since the king quite liked all this stuff, it was really an attack against him and the hierarchy that *he* represented.

NOT INVENTED YET. ED.

The majority of Parliament (like the majority of Englishmen) wanted to go at a reasonable pace with the reforms, but the fired-up minority wanted war and, as so often happens, the rest eventually got sucked in.

Time for another chapter.

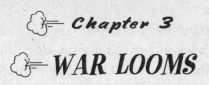

Chapter 3

WAR LOOMS

Civil wars and revolutions are often between the various classes – the poor always seem to be trying to overthrow the rich, and so on. Come to think of it, there wouldn't be much point the other way round, as the rich tend to have everything anyway, so why on earth would they have a go at the poor?* The English Civil War was different, basically being about religion and politics.

Most ordinary people found it difficult to know which way to jump – as always, there was right and wrong on both sides – but, as usual, their minds were made up for them by more powerful people who called the shots. Anyway, everyone either hoped that the king and the Parliamentarians would be able to talk their way out of a war before any blood was spilt, or at least believed that one good battle might settle the whole silly business.

The King's Side
It was all fairly predictable. The Roman Catholics, members of the High Church, most of the old duffers in the House of Lords and all those from the top drawer in society (mostly from country estates) all got behind the king (surprise, surprise). These Royalists were mostly from the North and the far South-West (Devon and Cornwall, etc.), and all in all, soldier-wise, raised 13,500 men.

---

* Brilliant deduction, Mr Farman. Ed

Parliament's Side

The Parliamentarians were supported by all those Puritans who'd been given such a hard time by the king, along with the members of the House of Commons. They were led by Robert Devereux, the Earl of Essex, a hugely popular and even hugelier* rich nobleman.

All the industrial areas (including the ports) and the navy (dead useful in wars and things) went against the king. The South and West, including London (by far the wealthiest city in the country), made up the bulk of their army. They managed to raise 15,000 men. All pretty even really.

War at Last

War was declared on 22 August 1642, but instead of getting down to it straight away, it was all a bit of an anticlimax, as the country seemed to just drift into turmoil. King Charles had left London in January to drum up support in the Midlands and the North – a slightly dodgy move, as it left all his best supporters in London and the surrounding counties without anywhere or anyone to rally round.

While he was up there, he and his men called in at Hull to grab the huge pile of weapons that had been left over from his somewhat pathetic attack on Scotland a few years earlier.

* 'Hugelier'??? Ed

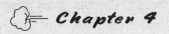
THE BATTLE OF  EDGEHILL, 1642

The Battle of Edgehill wasn't really planned. By October 1642 both armies were marching towards London, with the king and his Cavaliers in pursuit of the Earl of Essex and his Roundheads. There seemed, at the beginning, little chance of him and his men ever catching them up, unless Essex decided to stop and do his shoelaces up. As it happened, Essex's army was much larger and therefore slower than the king's, who was travelling light – not by choice, but because they had precious little equipment, no food, no tents and practically no armour. Both sides had really messed up on supplies and by the time they bumped into each other, almost accidentally, they were all exhausted and well fed up.

Close Encounter
In fact, a small bunch of Royalists literally ran into an even smaller bunch of Parliamentarians while they were both looking for billets (bed & breakfast to you) in the village of Wormleighton, and promptly captured them. This was the first

However, when he arrived at the city gates (they all had 'em in those days), despite much huffing and puffing, the doors remained locked and he and his men had to turn round, egg on face, and retire to York.

Useless Fact No. 894

Charles's wife, Henrietta Maria, might have been a bit of a liability but she certainly wasn't daft. She jumped on her hubby's warship, *Lion,* with all the crown jewels in her handbag. She was prepared to pawn the family sparklers to anyone who was prepared to help the Stuarts in their hour of need.

Useless Fact No. 895

As all this was going on, the member of Parliament for Huntingdon, a certain Oliver Cromwell (watch this name), had been busy. He'd gained many brownie points from his Parliamentary mates by hijacking a load of silver plate worth £21,000, a present from the university to the king. Cromwell quickly began to gather and train new troops. I bet the £21,000 helped!

clue for the king that the enemy were round the bend (or should I say round the corner). As they were so close, it seemed rather churlish not to have a battle – after all, that's what they'd come for.

Chief Roundhead Essex was apparently quite a cool customer. It turns out that he was actually on his way to church when he looked up and saw that the Royalists had gathered on the heights of Edge Hill and were pulling ugly faces at him and his men. Actually, Essex wasn't too wild about fighting that day (Sunday being his day off). He knew that the longer he hung around, the more likely it was that his other troops, over at Coventry and Warwick, might join him. He knew that if they were to fight now, the Cavaliers, led by the dashing Prince Rupert of Bavaria, would be stronger in cavalry (soldiers on horses), even if his Roundheads had far more guns. Young Rupert had kindly come over to England to help his uncle Charlie (who he'd heard was having a spot of bother).

Meanwhile . . .

At the church, Essex made his excuses to the vicar. He took his troops to the bottom of the hill and waited until three o'clock before trying out his guns. The Royalists responded and the battle was on. In those days muskets (long-barrelled guns) were only accurate up to a few metres and so nothing really happened (unless you count a load of banging) until the Cavalier cavalry charged.

Useless Fact No. 898

In the days before troops wore proper uniforms, the separate sides wore different coloured sashes to show who was who. This system was open to mass abuse as all one had to do was throw away one's sash and then no one knew who you belonged to. (I'd have had two sashes and I'd have shoved on the appropriate one as soon as I knew who was winning.*)

* Typical. Ed

Back at the Battle

Having nearly a thousand horses pounding down a hill towards you with a load of cross soldiers waving pistols and things is bound to induce a bit of nervousness. And Essex's horsemen were no exception. Quite understandably, they fired their carbines (short-barrelled guns used by the cavalry) off far too early, which meant that they failed to hit their targets. Caught short, they had to turn round and run for it, leaving the poor musketeers behind them, to be cut down at will.

The Roundhead pikemen (soldiers with smart spears), on the other hand, fared much better and soon had the upper hand over the Cavaliers, enabling *their* remaining cavalry to pick off the fleeing men. Suddenly the situation was reversed, and when the royal standard eventually got captured it looked as if the same fate might befall the king himself. By the evening, however, the soldiers were so exhausted and fed up with fighting that they simply stared at each other across the freezing battlefield strewn with dead and injured, wondering what to do next.

Useless Fact No. 901

Although the various armies were *led* by jolly rough, tough professional soldiers, who had all fought long and hard abroad, most of the men on both sides were simply volunteer farmers and labourers who were a bit of a joke when it came to the old fighting game.

Draw

When it came to the final body count, the Battle of Edgehill ended up almost even-Stevens, death-wise, with both sides having lost the same amount. In other words, a complete waste of time (let alone soldiers).

Time to Go

In the morning Essex peeked out of his tent, decided he didn't want to play any more and high-tailed it off with his troops towards London (their stronghold), approaching the city by the Great West Road (which wasn't there yet), passing Heathrow Airport (which wasn't there either). Much later, in 1643, the king's army followed and, realizing the capital's immense strategic importance, tried to take London from the west. But the Roundheads (and the Londoners) outnumbered them two to one. (To show how much they hated their king, 100,000 Londoners – men, women and children – helped build massive forts and ditches to keep him out.) The Royalists only got as far as Turnham Green before being stopped by the massive defences blocking their path. Without a shot being fired, Charles slunk back to Oxford, which became his wartime centre of operations.

Chapter 5

ANY MORE FOR ANY WAR?

At the same time as the king was making a mess of capturing his own capital, the Home Counties, the South and East, East Anglia and the Midlands fell under the control of the Parliamentarians. Not only that, but in the west and south of Yorkshire, the dead powerful Fairfaxes, who were also staunch supporters of Parliament, were preparing to prove their loyalty to the Earl of Essex. This left the Royalists with the North (both east and west), Cheshire and Lancashire, Wales and the Manchester area. As before, the West Country, right up to Dorset and Wiltshire, was Royalist. I think it fair to say that England was pretty equally divided.

No Peace

By December 1642 it became clear that the war was not going to go away – both sides refused to give in to the threats of the other. Every now and again, however, the two enemies would put out weedy little half-hearted requests for peace, withdrawing them as soon as the other side was rude to them.

Eastern Association

Another blow for the Royalists. Parliamentary opponents of the king representing Norfolk, Suffolk, Essex, Hertfordshire and Cambridgeshire decided to band together to form what was called the Eastern Association. Their aim was to make sure no Royalist groups caused any bother in their respective counties. Oliver Cromwell (keep watching out for this name), by the way, represented Cambridge.

Cash in Hand

Although the king had been unable to get back London, or its money, his funds weren't that bad. The sides, when you weighed everything up, were still sort of even, with the king having maybe a teeny-weeny advantage militarily. By the July of 1643, after a series of good wins over the Roundheads, the Cavaliers still held a slight advantage. Queen Henrietta Maria, now back from France with loads of cash, led her very own army to a surprise victory over Sir John Fairfax's Roundheads. This gained the king the whole of Yorkshire – apart from Hull.

Useless Fact No. 905

It was the women who made the most noise when it came to seeking peace. Parliament was blockaded by a huge mob of women demonstrators, which only broke up when the Roundhead cavalry waded in amongst them, killing several under their horses' hooves.

Scots Pitch In

All this Royalist success in England really got up the kilts of the Scots (still cross about that blasted Prayer Book) and they decided to help the Parliamentarians against Charles. But they didn't exactly *give* their services away – oh no, they charged the Parliamentarians a cool £30,000 a month for the rent of their army.

Ollie Looms Large

The Eastern Association hadn't seemed much cop when it started, but under the direction of its new Lieutenant-General, tough guy Oliver Cromwell (*still* keep watching for this name), it now became a force to be reckoned with, having an army of 20,000 highly trained and ever so tough Roundhead soldiers.

Oliver Cromwell*

Probably the most important character in the whole Civil War, Oliver Cromwell had come from quite a posh family in the county of Huntingdonshire (don't look on a map, it hasn't been there since 1974). He was quite a clever-clogs, by all accounts, and went to Cambridge University before returning to marry Sir James Bourchier's daughter, Elizabeth. By 1628 he was MP for the borough of Huntingdon, but when Parliament was dissolved by Charles in 1629 he had a go at farming – firstly at St Ives in Cornwall and later Ely in Cambridgeshire, where he'd inherited a large property. He now had a cosy private income, which allowed him to go off a-fighting whenever he wanted.

In the summer of 1642 he was called to recruit volunteers for the Parliamentary party and make them into soldiers. It was because of Cromwell that the super-professional Roundhead army of the Eastern Alliance became so powerful.

* Can we stop watching for this name now? Ed

The Battle of Marston Moor, 1644

Apart from Edgehill, most of the war had been a series of smallish bloody skirmishes rather than great big huge battles.

The Battle of Marston Moor (near York) was the largest and best battle in the Civil War.
Unfortunately Prince Rupert, leader of the cavalry, could only muster 15,000 men compared to the other side who'd by now pulled together three armies, including Cromwell's new and superb cavalry (the Ironsides) and the armies of the Scottish and English parliaments.
All in all *they* totalled 25,000. Pretty bad odds for the king, eh!

PRINCE RUPERT

Off We Go

Rupert started by relieving York which, although in Royalist hands, was under heavy siege from the Scots. He planned to attack the retreating Scottish army first thing in the morning but it took all day to get the armies up, dressed, breakfasted, and ready to go out to play, so when it came to the nitty-gritty they only really had an hour of daylight left for the scrap. Rupert said (in so many words), 'Blow this for a game of soldiers' and told his men to break for supper and get an early night ready for battle first thing in the morning.

As it turned out, it was a bad move. Oliver Cromwell was a smart cookie. He saw what was happening and, leading his fab new Ironsides cavalry, charged, just as the Cavaliers were tucking in (menu unknown). Rupert was understandably cross at having been disturbed during his tea and retaliated, causing a chunk of the Roundhead army to break up in disarray. But in the end Cromwell and the Scottish infantry and horsemen proved too strong and wrecked the Cavaliers' resolve (and their supper).

Night Fight

Luckily there was a full moon, for the fighting went backwards and forwards for hours. (It's so much better when you can see who you're fighting – and who's fighting you – don't you think?) The Roundheads got the better of it, and in the morning 3,000 Cavaliers were dead or dying on the pitch.* Cromwell, not known for his sense of humour, quipped, 'God made them as stubble to our swords,' which I presume was some kind of shaving joke.

Rupert was reckoned to have messed up badly, so he took his remaining men back to the safety of York. Read on, please.

---

* I think you mean 'battleground'. War isn't a game, you know. Ed
Oh no? JF

Chapter 6

CARRY ON FIGHTING

The Royalist cause was in a bad way after the goings-on at Marston Moor, but a few months later, in September 1644, the king cut off the Roundhead army and the Earl of Essex, forcing them first into Cornwall from Devon, and then onto the narrow peninsular of Fowey. Essex was stuck waiting for reinforcements to arrive by sea. But, typical of our tricky English weather, the wind changed and the boats, which were full of nice, freshly roundheaded soldiers, were blown back to where they came from. Essex knew the situation was pretty hopeless. He rowed out of Fowey harbour to a waiting ship, leaving the cavalry to make a run (or gallop) for it, and the poor army to surrender to Charles, who was well chuffed.

All in all, 6,000 Roundheads were now in his custody. That was the good news. The bad news came when he realized he'd probably have to feed the blighters. Cutting his losses, he freed the men but kept their weapons (isn't war ridiculous?*). The king now felt a little better about the situation but was still relying on his wife (didn't she turn out well!) to raise more help in France.

Meanwhile – in Scotland
The Royalists were also having a turn for the better up north. An army of 2,000 Irishmen were stumbling around the Highlands looking for a Royalist army to join up with. They were just about to walk right into the highly trained enemy

* This must be the first time I've ever agreed with you. Ed.

Covenanters' army when James Graham, Earl of Montrose, a major player in the Royalist cause (but at that particular time, armyless), got to them first. He was a known smooth-talker and to prove it he even got the nearby Covenanters' army to switch sides and join him. Nice work!

Together with the Irish they marched through Scotland defeating towns full of other Covenanters on the way. They eventually pitched up at Aberdeen in the North-East, which they took with a savagery that had never been seen before. Montrose then crossed Scotland again to ravage the lands of the Clan Campbell whose boss, the Marquess of Argyll, was more or less head of the Scottish government. This really hacked off his co-Parliamentarians, who sent a large Roundhead army specifically to catch Montrose. No way. In the depths of winter, he and his men made a remarkable march over the horrid heights of Lochaber and charged down on Argyll's army at Inverlochy.

Toy Soldiers?

The Parliamentarians, realizing the future lay with Cromwell, passed an Ordinance (a kind of Act) asking him to get together a complete army along the lines of his fabulous 'Ironside' cavalry (except not all with horses). The New Model Army consisted of:

 11 cavalry regiments of 600 riders

 12 foot regiments of 1,200

 1,000 dragoons (mounted soldiers with muskets)

Join our Club

There followed a string of stunning victories by the Roundheads, but by then the general public, who were, as always, caught bang (literally) in the middle, had had enough. In some areas the local population banded together, calling themselves (rather cosily, I think), the 'Clubmen'. They tried to drive out both sides, demanding that they negotiate an end to the wholesale destruction of their land (and their young men). That's not to mention the crippling taxation that Parliament had demanded in order to fight the war. The nation, they claimed, was 'bleeding under the devouring sword'. Many of the gentry whose estates fell within enemy territory had their property nicked, and if they didn't, they were forced to lend money to Parliament or the king depending on which side they were on. Not only that, but the population were expected to look after the wandering troops free of charge. Worse still, the soldiers paid them back by trampling all over their crops. Nice!

Useless Fact No. 909

There'd been a long-standing tiff between Cromwell and the haughty Earl of Manchester. Manchester reckoned Cromwell was a 'man of dangerous ideas' while Cromwell, a bit of a lefty, replied by saying that he hoped 'to live to see never a nobleman in England'. As they were the two natural choices to lead the New Model Army it was decided to ask an outsider instead, Sir Thomas Fairfax, just to avoid further squabbling.

Battle of Naseby

In June 1645 (the 14th to be precise)*, the king suffered his worst defeat yet when he came across the New Model Army under Fairfax at Naseby (Northamptonshire).

Ollie Cromwell was in charge of the cavalry as usual and together with the infantry they outnumbered the Cavaliers considerably.

Roundheads on Top

At first, the Royalist cavalry under the galloping Prince Rupert swept away the Ironside cavalry, but gradually the Roundheads started to get on top by sheer weight of numbers. Charles, seeing his army beginning to get the worst of things, turned his horse in order to charge in amongst the enemy. One of his men, realizing that they'd be on him like a pack of bloodthirsty hounds, snatched the king's bridle (well, the king's horse's bridle), pulling him away from the action. Unfortunately, the rest of the troops, seeing the king going the wrong way, reckoned this was a signal for them to run away too (any excuse). This action alone not only lost the battle, but maybe the whole blinking war.

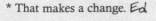 * That makes a change. Ed

Bad News for Charles

Despite Montrose's victories in Scotland, the overall picture in the North was not good for the king, the Covenanters having taken major Royalist strongholds like Carlisle and Scarborough. Charles began clutching at straws. His men were leaving him in droves on account of not being paid for ages (fickle or what?) and all attempts to get replacements were failing badly. He went first to Wales to raise foot soldiers, but they flatly refused to serve him. He even considered being nicer to Roman Catholics if they'd send him an army from Catholic Ireland. Actually, they said they would, but only if he allowed them to preach Catholicism openly and to let them hang on to any churches they managed to nick on the way.

'Oh dear, oh dear,' said Charles, 'it looks like I might have to do a deal with those nasty Scots Covenanters.' But that, he realized, would mean accepting Presbyterianism, which would never do. The Presbyterians, by the way, were rapidly falling out with the Parliamentarians. All very tricky. Let's face it, Charles mused, everyone *knew* God was a Protestant (including God) and that was all there was to it.

Useless Fact No. 911

It never rains but it pours. A load of letters that had been sent from Charles to the queen were found in a cabinet and then published. They showed that he had been thinking about bringing an army over from Ireland to fight the Parliamentarians, and that he was thinking of abolishing all the laws against Roman Catholics. This infuriated even the most loyal of his subjects.

Worse to Come

Probably the worst news in the war so far came when Charles heard that Montrose had finally been hit hard in the border area (ouch!) and that although the fearless leader had escaped, his whole Irish army and 300 camp followers had been executed on the orders of the Presbyterian clergy (the Lord moves in mysterious ways). Worse still, it turned out that Prince Rupert had surrendered the stronghold of Bristol to Fairfax (and Cromwell) which made the king so mad that he fired Rupert from his command.

To balance all this, however, all over the country the Parliamentarian troops, also fed up with fighting for no money, hungry and reduced to rags, were beginning to mutiny. Parliament was hopelessly in debt to the city of London, the Scots and a thousand other creditors to the tune of £2.5 million pounds (£180 million in today's money).

Useless Fact No. 913

The soldiers were so hungry that they were literally eating farm animals in front of their helpless owners. I suppose it could have been worse – it could have been the other way round.*

Charles Gives In

This is where it all gets a bit weird. A strange man with short hair, a funny accent and an extremely dodgy beard (Rolf Harris?) pitched up at the Saracen's Head at Southwell in Nottinghamshire, asking to make contact with the Scottish army's headquarters nearby. Poor old Charles, for it was he (as if you hadn't guessed), was seeking protective custody with the Scots and if they refused (which they didn't) he was going to

* Don't be silly. Ed

flee the country to join either his missus or his son Charles (one day to be II) who were in France and Jersey respectively. He had been posing as the servant of his chaplain – a certain Dr Hudson – and had escaped from his headquarters in Oxford which was now under siege from the Roundheads.

Power Pledge

In order to win this damnable war once and for all, the Parliamentarians had to do two things.

For a start they gave away some of their mighty powers to a series of committees in London, who in turn dished more out to a lot of committees throughout the counties and regions. These new powers – like looking into people's wealth, searching their houses, even taking their goods at will – were nothing less than outrageous and carried far greater weight than the actual law of the land.

Better still (depending on whose side you were on), these committees were above any future repercussions; in other words – above the law for ever.

The ridiculous thing was that this new government had become far worse than the one before (the king's) that they'd been moaning about in the first place (and we all know what that feels like).

Scots' Promise

Oh boy, were those Parliamentarians sneaky. They promised the Scots that if they'd stay on their side, they'd reform their own church and make it a Presbyterian one. To be honest, that's not exactly what they said, but the wording was so clever that that was what the Scots thought that was what they said. (All clear?) They promised to get rid of bishops (again!!!), cathedrals, church courts and the Book of Common Prayer (replacing it with a Directory of Worship). There were, of course, many objections on both sides. The dissenters in the English parliament produced a list of objections so long that they were only allowed to print the first 300.

Persuading the King

King Charles was being held (gently) by the Scots at Newcastle and for months they tried their level best to get him to accept Presbyterianism – which would probably have ended the war. But Charles knew that if he agreed to these 'Newcastle Propositions', he'd be playing into the Parliamentarians' hands: as well as completely changing his religious ideology, it would reduce his power – and *that* would never do.

Cut-Price King

Charles kept them guessing for months, which made the Scots angrier and angrier. Little did he know that while this was going on, Parliament was negotiating to buy him off his keepers – the Scots – who agreed to go back home when they got the cash (just imagine selling the Queen!*). The price was £400,000, to be paid in two instalments, and when they eventually handed poor old Charlie over in February 1647 they dutifully marched back home after having occupied bits of England for four years.

* Don't even go there. Ed

Chapter 7

1647: CHARLES MAKES A COMEBACK

You might have thought that Charles would have sneaked back to England to avoid the wrath of his subjects, but not a bit of it. All along the route, church bells cheered and crowds pealed.* At Nottingham, Sir Thomas Fairfax (Black Tom), who'd spent the last goodness-knows-how-long trying to stitch Charles up, rode out and kissed the king's hand, while local landowners turned out in their thousands to welcome him and accompany him back to London.

This, as you can imagine, gave the king fresh hope that his war-weary people would have him back on his old terms. His subjects, however, despite their affection for him, thought somewhat differently. Surely dear old God wouldn't have put his faithful flock through such hard times for nothing. If they went straight back to worshipping in the way they had *before* all this kerfuffle occurred, it would be an insult to all those who had died – they thought.

The End?

Ending a war is always more difficult than starting one. The New Model Army, for instance, supported by their leader, Cromwell, demanded loads of back pay and refused to disband until their Roundhead bosses coughed up. Parliament was totally penniless and realized that there was not a single penny

* No they didn't. Ed

of extra taxation to be squeezed out of a people who had long known that the bloody Civil War had achieved next to nothing.

The Army Takes Over

By August of 1647 London was under a kind of martial law (i.e. governed by the army). The New Model Army, led by Fairfax and Cromwell, had marched into the city, pulled out all the troublesome independents from Parliament (thus making it totally illegal) and threatened the rest into voting to stump up the cash due to the army. They also ignored the pleas of a large group called 'the Levellers' . . .

OLIVER CROMWELL

The Levellers

The Levellers wanted to dissolve Parliament, declare all existing government null and void and start afresh with a new democratic constitution. They also wanted all Englishmen to sign a sort of social contract or 'Agreement of the People' and to be part of a democratic and decentralized state. People in authority should only keep the jobs for a short period and, most important of all, anyone under the Levellers' regime should be able to worship who and how they pleased – as long as they were Christian. (Like Henry Ford saying that the public could have any colour car they wanted – as long as it was black.) The Levellers were the first to even *suggest* equal rights for women, and a fair education for all.

Oddly enough, their ideas rather appealed to the army chiefs (nicknamed 'grandees'). After much discussion (the Putney Debates), however, which at one point looked as though there *could* be an agreement between the Levellers, the New Model Army and the king, they finally decided otherwise. Good as the theory of a one-man/one-vote constitution might be, the whole set-up would go no way towards helping the soldiers get back their hard-earned dosh. And that, when it came right down to it, was all they really cared about.

Infighting

Meanwhile, General Cromwell had set up home in the Tower and the rest of the army ringed London in preparation for a siege. The king, still in close arrest, was having a right hoot over this major tiff between Parliament and what had once been its own army and, enjoying this new situation, flatly refused a set of new and quite reasonable proposals put to him by Sir Thomas Fairfax.

Parliament was now totally discredited and Fairfax gave orders for 18,000 troops to march with Cromwell to 'purge and purge and purge the Commons.'

Up to His Old Tricks

Few doubted how tricksy and clever King Charles I could be, especially when it came to his own survival, but no one seriously imagined that he could even consider reviving the Royalist cause. But Charlie was a cunning old dog and one day simply disappeared from house arrest at Hampton Court, leaving no clue as to where he'd gone.

The nation naturally went into panic mode, suspecting some kind of plot. Black Tom Fairfax (still head of the army) got nearest to the truth, reckoning that the king had

gone north to parley with the Scots. Close, but not close enough.

Clever Charles had fooled them all by arranging to meet the Scots, not in Scotland, but at his castle on the Isle of Wight – far from the grasp of Parliament or the army. Meanwhile, just to make the whole business all the more complicated, the Irish in Ireland* rose in rebellion against the Protestants in general.

Wheeling and Dealing

But Charles was soon doing secret deals with Scottish noblemen, promising that in return for their military support he would make all of England and Ireland Presbyterian for a three-year trial period (here we go again!!), even though he wouldn't actually go down that road himself (he must have kept his fingers crossed behind his back throughout all the negotiations).

In January 1648, when Parliament found out what Charles had been up to, they broke off all communications with him

* Where else would they be? Ed.
England? JF

and threatened death to anyone else who even tried. They'd been well and truly double-crossed and they weren't too happy about it, to say the least. In fact, they were really out to get him this time. What a situation . . . (And we think relations between the Royals and government are frosty these days!)

The Second Civil War

Just as all this was going on, a full-scale war was emerging in most of the areas that hadn't had a proper war before (amongst those who hadn't yet become completely disgusted by it all). It was a revolt of the provinces against military rule, and against the power of the central government, who were always interfering with their lives. It was led by all the more moderate Parliamentarians and the Clubmen (remember them?), encouraged by all those ex-Royalists who didn't have much else to do.

Meanwhile . . .

The deal struck between Charles and the Scottish noblemen (called 'the Engagement') on the Isle of Wight in December 1647 had thrown the Scots into confusion. They accused the Duke of Hamilton, a close mate of the king's and leader of the Scottish delegation, of being an England-lover, which was one of the worst things you could say to a Scot (still is!). The mighty Scottish chieftains who made up the Kirk (the Scottish church) then threw out the Engagement as being a dreadful betrayal of the Covenant.

Useless Fact No. 917

The poor old Duke of Hamilton lived to regret the deal he made with the king, for only three months later he lost his head somewhere in London, for being on the wrong side.

The chaps who negotiated with the king, the 'Engagers', controlled the Scottish Parliament at the time, but the Kirk held far more real power and was able to ruin or at least severely mess up their attempts to get together an army to invade England. It became almost impossible to raise a decent army and in the end it was only 15,000 ill-trained and ill-equipped Scottish troops who crossed the border.

CAN I HAVE A GO OF YOUR SWORD WHEN YOU'VE FINISHED?

Cromwell Triumphs

Needless to say, Hamilton's Engager army of brave but badly trained Scotsmen was totally overwhelmed by Cromwell's immaculate Model Army at the Battle of Preston, in August 1648. Loads of them surrendered before risking so much as a cut finger. The following month saw the Engager government collapse, with Cromwell driving them from office. They were replaced by the Covenanters or 'Whigs'.

Useless Fact No. 919
The word 'whig' is said to come from 'whiggam', which means 'to spur on a horse'.

The new boys had no love for old Cromwell or his army, but they didn't really have a lot of choice when you come to think of it. By the way, the Second Civil War was now officially over, with nothing whatsoever achieved. It was more or less back to square one.

Pride's Purge

The army acted quickly when they heard that Charles was now on the verge of doing a deal with Parliament that would release him from any responsibility for the Civil War and therefore deny the possibility of his being treed for trison.* In December 1648, a chap called Colonel Pride was put in charge of a guard on Parliament House, halting any Presbyterians who wanted to get in, and arresting 140 of its members. The 60 who were left, called 'the Rump', were the ones that were as good as guaranteed to take steps against the king.

* I think you mean 'tried for treason'. Ed

Chapter 8

≋ *A PAIN IN THE NECK*

On 1 December 1648 poor old Charles was moved from the rather charming Carisbrook Castle to the extremely horrid Hurst Castle on a bleak headland in Hampshire. Mind you, it could have been worse – he still had nine servants and three cooks (which is far more than I've got*). By the following January, a high court had been appointed to try the king, but it was little more than a formality. Charles had been brought to London and on to Westminster by barge. Brave and stroppy to the last, he refused to remove his tall, black hat. Actually, he soon wouldn't have a head to put it on anyway. (Sorry to give the end away – again.)

He also refused to recognize the court and stayed silent during the questioning. It was as good as committing suicide. Had he pleaded 'not guilty' it would have taken months to produce a case (you know what lawyers are like) and in that time his mates from all over Europe would have been certain to come to his aid with far more than words.

* You haven't got any. Ed
Exactly. JF

Death to the King

On 27 January 1649, he was condemned to death for high treason: 59 soldiers led by Oliver Cromwell signed the death warrant. General Fairfax, who respected the king despite having fought against him, refused, and his wife even yelled out in the king's defence throughout the proceedings.

Three days later Charles I was taken to Whitehall to be executed. Before going out into the cold winter air, he asked to wear two shirts as he didn't want the punters to think he was shivering from fear. As his head plopped into the basket, a howl went up from the crowd. What had they done? It was the first time a king of England had been executed by his own subjects.

Oliver Cromwell, surprise, surprise, couldn't join the fun. He was too busy in the House of Commons making sure an act was passed preventing Charles's lad (Charles) from succeeding him. The Scots, a wee bit annoyed at having their king disposed of without being asked (and by the English), supported the heir to the throne, but – true to form – only if he promised to restore Presbyterianism in England and Scotland. Talk about playing an old tune on old bagpipes.

A Bit About Charles II

Young Charles was only 19 when his dad was topped and the Scots told him he was their new king. He'd been living in the Hague with William of Orange. He was much better built and taller than his dad (even *with* his head on) and not shy and tongue-tied as poor old Charles I had been.

No More Monarchy

On 7 February the 'Rump' parliament decided, as everyone knew they would, to get rid of the monarchy and the House of

Lords in one clean sweep. By May 1649 England was a republican state (never before or since seen in England, unfortunately*), but it's fair to say that the English, still trying to scour their king's blood from their hands, were less than deliriously happy about it.

Ollie has Fun

Oliver Cromwell, now by far the most powerful guy in the country, then took a little time off to do what he liked doing best – crushing and destroying those weaker than himself. In September 1649 he crossed to Ireland with 12,000 of his toughest bully boys and totally trashed the Catholic rebellion that had been going on for eight years or so. Cromwell's methods were the most vicious and disgusting seen to date. It was simple: destroy all clergy, landowners and soldiers – 2,600 in all – and then make the country Protestant. Job done. Return home, tired but happy.

Useless Fact No. 921
Cromwell, in order to get the best out of his lads, didn't leave Bristol for Ireland until every penny of their back pay had been distributed.

Oliver came back to a hero's welcome in June 1650, having removed that nasty little Irish Catholic thorn from England's side, and was promptly made Commander-in-Chief of all Commonwealth Forces as a kind of thank-you present.

Useless Fact No. 924
From 1649–1660, the Commonwealth was the name given to Parliament.

* We'll have none of your republican thoughts here, Mr Farman. Ed

Useless Fact No. 925

One of the English movements that Cromwell was determined to tackle (as well as the anti-war Levellers and the anti-military Quakers) was called the 'Ranters', a rather jolly and decidedly modern bunch, who believed that there was nothing wrong with drunkenness, sexual promiscuity or general immoral behaviour. In fact, they went as far as saying that sin didn't exist, a theory that showed signs of being very popular indeed, especially with the poor (and who can blame them). I wonder if that's where the expression 'ranting and raving' comes from?

Young Charles Hides Out

Charles was in Paris with his French mum, Maria, when he heard about Cromwell's success in Ireland. He'd apparently had a tiff with Mum and moved to Jersey, but heard no more of the goings-on back home. When he finally got to Scotland in the June of 1650, he heard what was about to happen to the captured Montrose (coming soon) but refused to do anything about it, an act that was to give him a black mark that stayed with him for ages. He then went to stay at his palace at

Dunfermline but was kept a virtual prisoner by his strictly religious hosts, who made him pray all day and even worse, kept delaying his coronation.

Scotland Next

Flushed with his success in Ireland, Oliver Cromwell then decided to have a go at the Scots, who were still Royalists (remember?), before *they* had a go at the English (who weren't). Cromwell wanted Fairfax to lead the campaign, but old Fairfax, still unhappy about the execution of the king, refused, claiming it was unethical.

Cromwell, therefore, led the troops himself, but had a frustrating time in the September of 1650 chasing the Scots round the Highlands (the spoilsports seemed to be refusing to fight). When he decided to give up and go home, the Scots interpreted this as a retreat, and went after him with 26,000 soldiers. They should have beaten Oliver's 11,000 men (all that were left after a terrible attack of fever) hands down, but canny Cromwell decide to attack before they were quite ready (four o'clock-in-the-morning-not-ready), just as he'd done at the battle of Marston Moor (old rabbits die hard*). It was a complete rout, killing 4,000 Scots (many in their tents) and capturing a further 10,000. There was no stopping him.

Montrose Goes Four Ways

Just to show how much they meant business, on 21 May, the Marquis of Montrose (the brave soldier who'd fought for Charles I in Scotland) was hung in Edinburgh, on a scaffold an unprecedented 10 metres from the ground. (Actually, I wouldn't have thought it made much difference how high you were hung. Dead's dead.) Swashbuckling to the last, he joked all the way to his death.

Useless Fact No. 927

After a few hours Montrose's body was cut down, and his head removed. Then, just for the hell of it, he was cut into four quarters and his head stuck on a pike on the Edinburgh Tolbooth. And for good measure, his four limbs were sent to the town gates of Stirling, Glasgow, Perth and Aberdeen. It's good to travel.

On 1 January 1651 Charles II was finally crowned King of England, Scotland and Ireland, having apologized for the behaviour of his mum and dad – but even as the ceremony was going on, old Cromwell was advancing again. Young Charlie had to recruit more soldiers – and quick. By the time of his birthday on 19 May he'd raised 19,000 men, including English veterans from the Civil War who'd remained Presbyterian.

To cut a long story (and a load of Scottish soldiers) short, Cromwell was again too strong for them. Charles had decided to attack south of the border, leaving Ollie's Roundhead army *behind* him in Scotland. Cromwell thought this was brill because the Scots and Charlie were now trapped in England. He could drive them like sheep into a pen.

* I think you mean 'habits'. Ed

The Scottish soldiers, who hadn't thought they'd signed up to fight in England, were well fed up and began to peel off and trudge home. By the time the king reached Worcester he only had 12,000 men left as opposed to Cromwell's 30,000. Now it doesn't take a genius to work out that 12,000 vs. 30,000 is not a fair fight, and it doesn't take a crystal ball to work out who was likely to win. Oddly enough, this time Cromwell wanted as few deaths as poss, apart from the king: 'For me, it is a crown or a coffin,' he said. (Another weedy Roundhead joke.)

In the end, thousands of the Scottish infantry surrendered, while their cavalry galloped back towards Scotland. The young king, realizing the game was up, then camouflaged his face, put on old clothes and slunk away to Worcester where he hid up a tree in the middle of a field for a bit (as you do). He then decided to take a little boat on a long trip from Brighton to France, disguised as the servant of Jane Lang, the sister of one of his colonels. The struggle that had raged since 1642 was now finally over and all that was left was for Cromwell's top man General Monck to clear up all the Scottish strongholds that still refused to accept the inevitable.

By January of 1652, English commissioners had taken over the government of Scotland, and the two countries were made one.

Useless but Interesting Fact No. 929

That nasty Mr Hitler's soldiers weren't the first to march in that ridiculous goosestep-style. The nursery rhyme *Goosey, Goosey Gander* refers to Cromwell's army, who were trained to march in goosestep while searching for Cavalier fugitives.

> *Goosey, goosey gander,*
> *Whither shall I wander?*
> *Upstairs and downstairs*
> *And in my lady's chamber.*
> *There I met an old man*
> *Who would not say his prayers,*
> *I took him by the left leg*
> *And threw him down the stairs.*

Nobody seems to know who the old lady was, but I bet the poor old geezer who took the tumble was someone who wouldn't switch to the strict Puritan way of praying.

Chapter 9

HOW IT ALL TURNED OUT

Charles II was in France with a tag of *£1,000 Dead or Alive* on his noble head, but there were no extradition agreements* in those days so he was fairly safe.

Cromwell led a bunch of his best musketeers to Parliament and dissolved the 'Rump' of the Long Parliament, which had been sitting for over twelve and a half years (I expect they could have done with a break). As you can imagine, there was an awful situation developing between the army and Parliament and there were calls for fresh elections. The members then tried to rush through a 'perpetual bill' which meant they could keep their seats for ever – quite a smart idea. Oliver dealt with it in his own inimitable way, by denouncing the proceedings, grabbing the mace and telling his own soldiers to empty the chamber and take the 'bauble' away. He then set up what became jokingly known as a 'bare bones parliament', which was nominated rather than elected.

King Ollie I?

After only four months, this parliament dissolved itself and handed over all power to Cromwell, who became Lord Protector, having turned up his rather huge nose at being king. As it was, he was the first 'commoner' before or since to rule the country. Cromwell had had no qualms about executing King Charles I. As far as he was concerned he was simply

---

* I'll explain. An extradition agreement means that a country will hand over a person accused of a crime to the country that's accusing him or her. Ed

doing what God wanted. Neither did he give a fig for civil and legal liberties; he governed simply as the mood took him. If he wanted a man in jail, he jailed him. If he needed more money he invented new taxes (a bit like the king had tried to do a few years before). Therefore, when he was offered the throne, he refused it, cleverly realizing that accepting it would reduce his power. Even kings sometimes have to listen to their advisors and usually have to obey the law.

Useless Fact No. 932

Two Royalists, John Gerard and Peter Vowell, were beheaded on 10 July for conspiring to kill Cromwell. Two of their co-conspirators were sent to Barbados, which might sound all right to you, but in those days it was a slave island.

Cromwell Rules OK

Cromwell *was* the law. As far as he was concerned, if God had wanted him to make moves to become king, He'd have told him. He didn't, so naturally he didn't either.

While Cromwell was alive, he kept the army (who had the physical muscle) and the landed gentry (who had the power, socially speaking) apart. He (Cromwell) was the only link between them, being a funny mixture of country gent and soldier. He was the only real stability on the one hand and, if you think about it, the source of potential instability on the other. In other words, the future was all up to him.

Cromwell Dies

Shock horror, talk about a spanner in the works! On 3 September 1658, Ollie the Great, Lord Protector of all England, died. Being a closet softie at heart (despite being a ruthless killer up front), he had never quite recovered from the death of his daughter, Bessie, and had been sick for some time. Too weak to even speak, he simply nodded when asked if it would be all right for his only surviving son, Richard (he'd had three), to take over the job. Knowing what his son was like, he was probably only trying to ask for a glass of water . . . but Richard got the job, anyway.

Poor Dick

Well sort of! Oh dear, oh dear, 'Tumbledown Dick' (as he was unaffectionately known) was in no way like his dad – and no match for the army, who weren't prepared to be ruled by civil power. Led by a General John Lambert, Richard Cromwell was forced to dissolve Parliament, but was allowed to keep his job as long as he kept his mouth shut.

Return of the Rump

The army, of course, was useless at country-running (as all armies ever have been) and only a month later begged the old 'Rump' parliament (that had been kicked out so ignominiously by Oliver Cromwell) to return.

But the feud between the army and the 45-strong (or weak) parliament continued to the point that another civil war looked possible. Army chief General Lambert even blockaded the House of Commons, refusing to let any of the members in.

On 12th October the Rump reacted. They chucked out the job of Commander-in-Chief, fired Lambert and pushed poor Richard even deeper into the shadows. But the army wasn't done for yet. Headed by Lambert they retaliated by suggesting the return of the king (can you believe it?) with the General himself as the power behind the throne.

At this point, the mighty General Monck, who was still giving it plenty up in Scotland, declared himself to be a strong supporter of the Rump (are you following all this?) and by so saying neatly divided the army against itself. Three months later he returned triumphantly to London, dissolved the Rump with their blessing and called for a free parliament, including all those kicked out during Colonel Pride's Purge twelve years earlier (see page 50). As he'd marched south through the happy thronging crowds, he was left in no doubt that the country not only wanted their old parliament back, but also a proper king again.

The Restoration of the Monarchy

On 29 May 1660 King Charles II entered London with 100,000 people who'd accompanied him all the way from Dover, where he had landed from France. England had what was probably the biggest party to date. The Civil Wars were now, thank God, a thing of the past. So was Puritanism. And so is this book.

Useless Fact No. 935

Just as a parting shot, Oliver Cromwell, who'd died peacefully two years earlier, was dug up and formally hung. As if that wasn't enough for an old, smelly corpse, it was then cut down and beheaded.

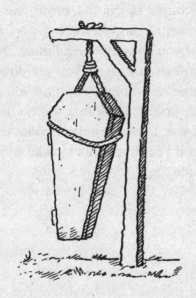

⟨⟩ TIME'S UP

There you are, I've done it again. The history of the Civil War in under sixty-four pages (with piccies), even with my grumpy editor nipping at my heels.* I'd be lying if I didn't admit that I've somewhat simplified the whole sorry business, but I expect you've got other things to do. Anyway, what more do you want for a couple of quid? I mean, we don't want to become anoraks over all this, do we?

But seriously, if you do want to read more about Cromwell, or the King Charleses, I suggest you get down to the local library and ask that nice librarian to find you some more on the subject. While you're doing that, I'll no doubt be writing about something else. In the meantime, folks, try to keep clear of civil wars – but if you simply can't, make sure you're always on the winning side . . .

---

* Grumpy? Me, *grumpy?* Ed